LITTLE BOOK
OF
BiG
LESSONS

VOLUME 1

JAMIE THOMPSON

Little Book of Big Lessons
© 2022 Jamie Thompson

ISBN 978-1-66786-835-6
eBook ISBN 978-1-66786-836-3

To my children, with love.
You are my inspiration and motivation.

Pierre, my love, my son. Firstborn and only son. My heart began to heal as soon as I heard yours beat for the first time. Thank you for giving me a reason to push past the failures and disappointments in life and press toward the place God prepared for us. You have grown into a man to admire, respect, and honor. You remind me of who and whose I am, and that there is no limit other than the ones we create. Your life is a testament to faith with works. Never stop praying, dreaming, believing, and doing.

Jamie, my first daughter, God's anointed one. You are everything I am and not. You are the part of me that is untouched, pure, free, and innocent, the part of me I let go of too fast and too soon. Thank you for teaching me the power of "different." You show me daily what a life surrendered totally unto the Lord looks like. You are beautiful inside and out. The rarest and fairest of them all. You are my accountability piece and standard of favored femininity that I have yet to see in another. If the woman described in Proverbs 31 were a portrait, we would see you. Continue to embrace God as he keeps carrying you and lifting you up with his righteous hand. You are royalty and truly seated in heavenly places.

Jasiah, my faith, my strength. You have taught me to trust God in ways I could have never imagined. You teach anyone willing to learn that we all have a voice. As I watch you, I have learned that we can say more with our eyes, smile, and presence than we can with our words. Your spirit and understanding reveal the mysteries of God. God said that He uses the foolish to put the wise to shame and the weak things of this world to put the powerful to shame; you are proof of these words. Thank you for your contagious laugh and smile that radiates love and joy, along with pure praise and worship that beckons angels to join you.

Ja'Dore, my beautiful dreamer. The perfect gift to our family. You are love; you are light; you are beauty; you are power; you are joy; you are adored. You are the perfect balance of soft and strong, classic, and modern, wealthy, and humble. You have the gift of healing, the gift of helping, and a voice anointed to speak and command change. You have been given a double portion of wisdom, love, and discernment. You remind me that the power of gentleness can make the hardest of hearts soft again. Your greatest gift is your authentic self. Never change who you are to fit into a place not big enough to contain you. BeYOUtiful.

TABLE OF CONTENTS

DEDICATION

This book is dedicated to every person who has realized that you have poured out more of yourself than you have poured into yourself. You have been living and doing life as your heart led. Now suddenly, you are looking around at the lives of those you have touched and realize that they have been living and you have simply been doing.

Let me say this: you are not alone, and it is okay. No matter how old you are and where you currently are in life, being aware is the first step toward being alive and living. Now that you have taken the time to pause long enough to check your own pulse, you can begin to apply what you have learned throughout your journey in life to refuel, renew, and readjust.

NOTE

I am not currently a licensed therapist. I am simply a woman who has been given the gift of love from our creator. People are my passion, and the thoughts I have been led to share come from my heart, the heart that my personal life experiences have shaped.

I am not attempting to provide advice, but merely my perspective. As you read, we may not always agree, but my hope is that something is shared that will promote the power of pause. The power of pause allows us to consider our thoughts, feelings, and possible actions. It allows us to move on purpose, with purpose.

Know this: only you can rediscover yourself, but I would like to share some nuggets of wisdom that I have collected along my journey. Things I discovered about myself, people I have encountered along the way, and other things that I am grateful to know. Again, I imagine you will not agree with or like everything I may say, but I hope that something I share makes your road a little easier, perhaps makes you think, smile, laugh, or cry. But mainly, my desire is to inspire.

Inspire you to take a step back, push pause on people, and take the time to press play on yourself. Get to know who you are, what you like, what you need, and what you want. Discover what is negotiable and what is unacceptable to you. It is wise to know this now without heart fog, an expression I use when we are unable to see clearly in a situation due to emotional scales hindering our sight. Once this is known, you can take the time to appreciate who you are and become comfortable and confident in your truth. After reaching this point, you can walk confidently in the direction you are being led to go.

Now let's begin!

LITTLE LESSONS, BIG CHANGE

The truth hurts,
but a lie is worse.
Sadly, both may cost the
same—everything.

BEYOUTIFUL!

When I was younger, I would adapt to the person I was dating. Not only would I adapt, but I would also begin to change according to what was appealing to the person. I yearned to be liked, loved, and valued. I thought changing myself would increase their level of attraction toward me. However, no matter how many people would compliment me or how often my smile would move someone toward me, I was unable to see what they saw. Do not get me wrong. I saw the blanket of beauty and scarf of sex appeal, but I lacked self-love and confidence. I did not believe anyone could love me unconditionally, just for me. I am not sure if anyone knew this about me during that season in my life because I would typically mask the insecurity with false arrogance.

After years of learning and growing through my experiences, I finally realized that I was not using my greatest gift: myself. I looked around and realized that nobody knew me. I did not know myself. I always attempted to accept everyone for who they were, even while hoping change would come in time. Yet, it took thirty-five years for me to finally take off the mask. I took time off from dating to discover who I was. I was not just a pretty girl with dimples. I was not the loud, fast, slick-talking little girl my father called me. I was not "miss know-it-all" as my family would call me. I was not "mean and stubborn" as guys would say. I was not "arrogant" or "stuck-up" as females would say. No, I learned I am a woman of faith; I love and trust God. I am strong but sensitive. I am smart and wise, with still much to learn. I am passionate and compassionate. Resilient and adaptable. Determined and persistent. Romantic but not gullible. Caring, with a heart of a servant leader. More beautiful on the inside than outwardly. Deeper than the earth's core but lighter than a blade of grass.

I am loyal and honest.

Transparent and free. I am creative, generous, encouraging, discerning, imaginative, and positive. I am an optimistic realist. I am a loving and supportive mother, a trusting friend, a discrete counselor, and an accountable partner. I am an effective communicator who loves people. I am me! I love myself! What you see is what you get. Know this: the best and most lasting love will know all of you and love you despite you.

Who are you?

ONE DAY, ONE MOMENT, ONE DECISION AT A TIME.

I have the unfortunate tendency to overthink things. I can think so far into the future that I miss what is going on now, which sometimes causes me to fall for or hold onto potential rather than understand reality.

Avoid walking through life with your eyes wide shut. Look at things as they are without your interpretation. Be quiet and listen closely to the things being said through the vibrations in and around you. Imagination is great; it creates new ideas. However, missing reality may hinder progress. Today, this moment is all we have; tomorrow may never come. If it does, we are unable to enjoy the hope of tomorrow without living through today. See what is in front of you now. Stop making excuses for what you see. If someone says one thing but does another, call it out. If they never answer a call but always seem to be able to text, and that bothers you, say something. If they only seem to be able to talk to you or see you at a specific time, do not sit and drive yourself crazy wondering. Instead, take the time and ask why.

Many times, if our heart is afraid of the truth that our spirit has already discerned and accepted, we do not ask the necessary questions. Instead, we simply allow our imagination to fill in the blanks in a manner that fits our immediate desire, which seems especially true when lust is involved.

Remember, the Bible says that the heart is deceptive.

Avoid deceiving yourself. You can be open and walk circumspectly at the same time. I call myself an optimistic realist. Yes, I said it. The word realist often carries a negative connotation. It is as if a realist must be pessimistic. However, a realist simply sees a situation for what it is and is prepared to deal with it accordingly. Being optimistic is simply being hopeful and confident about the future. I am both. I see and deal with things accordingly while persevering through whatever it may be because I am hopeful and confident about the future. Never allow others to put you in the box they have created for you.

Be fluid. Be unique. Be you without limitations.

Love yourself and others will follow your example.

ONE AT A TIME, TRUST ME!

After six years of celibacy, as soon as I confessed with my mouth that I was ready to begin dating, I met two all-around good men within days of one another. After several conversations with each, I went on two dates with one and sincerely enjoyed the time we spent. We had quite a bit in common, especially in areas most important to me. I went out once with the other and found him intriguing, poised, rugged, smart, and very confident. He also challenged my perspective on a few things. I liked him as well and wanted to know more about each of them.

I sincerely thought, *hey, I am dating. I am not in a relationship, and it is all brand new.* At this point, I was still getting to know them. I was challenged by a friend to focus on one individual at a time to avoid falling for two people, potentially hurting someone, or being hurt. I agreed and cut it off with the man I thought I had less in common with.

Whether you agree with my decision or not, just know that it is quite difficult to get to know someone and give a potential relationship a fair chance while dating multiple people. You will always find yourself comparing one to the other, becoming more of a judge in a competition rather than finding an opportunity to build an authentic and lasting relationship if that is what you sincerely desire.

As women, we must understand that men also have feelings, expectations, and desires to have a meaningful relationship with someone they can trust. Many men deal with abandonment and trust issues, not to mention various insecurities and other dysfunctions stemming from childhood that were left unresolved. Sadly, in many cultures, men are taught to be strong, keep their feelings to themselves, and above all, not cry.

This unfortunate way of thinking has seemingly hindered black men's emotional intelligence, while also impacting how couples communicate, making it difficult for many couples to connect on a deeper level that could potentially cultivate a path to marriage.

Without the help of counseling, a word that has been taboo in the black community, many men struggle with expressing their feelings, fearful of being seen as weak, spineless, a pushover.

We have a responsibility to ourselves and others to be honest, direct, and sincere about who we are, what we desire, and what we can give. Trust that there's always a choice, and there will always be a consequence for our choices. However, we must remember that we do not get a choice in the consequences we must face after making our decisions.

Take time to choose wisely!

Relationships are like bank accounts. We must make deposits before withdrawals, or we end up with a negative balance.

THERE IS WISDOM
IN COUNSEL.

I thought I had it all figured out. I was wise for my age, had attained knowledge, and had experienced a lot in a short amount of time.

Before marriage, I participated in pre-marital counseling. However, I did not communicate the depths of my heart. I thought I knew enough to get through anything. I was also afraid to hear the feedback that may be communicated to me about me if I shared my thoughts, concerns, and situations that had taken place previously. I did not use the tools that I was provided and did not seek wisdom. I married for all the wrong reasons and without true knowledge of the person I became one with. I did not ask the right questions. I made a long-term decision based on temporary emotions.

Remember, no matter how much you know or how much you have seen, there is always more to learn. Read books, browse articles, and ask other experienced individuals about their lives. The more we know, the more we grow.

While dating, I urge everyone to ask tough questions, questions that matter. While you are single, take the time to discover your needs and wants. Not necessarily an actual list, but an internal list in your heart. Needs would be non-negotiable areas in your life. Perhaps questions regarding faith, children, finances, and future goals. Yes, consider your future goals. When considering a life partner, consider your whole life, not only the present. No, we cannot predict what is to come, but we know what we want and are working towards. The Bible says, "Two cannot walk together except they agreed." (NIV)

As we go and grow through life, we want to grow together with our partners. Wants would be the more superficial desires—height, weight, complexion, educational background, and the like.

Discuss the complex and important areas first to avoid wasting time. If the most important values, goals, and desires are not discussed, then the interaction is more than likely led by lust or other superficial reasons. If the other person is unwilling to disclose information within a reasonable amount of time, move on. If you do not, you will find yourself surviving in a relationship of compromise instead of living.

You were created as a masterpiece, not just a piece (of meat).

NEGLECTING YOURSELF IS NOT A REQUIREMENT FOR LOVE.

When someone is new and interesting to us, we want to know everything about them. So, we spend numerous hours talking, texting, and even video chatting. We may even begin to deviate from our normal routines. As women, we seem to have the tendency to prioritize this new person even before securing a position in their life. By doing this, we begin to neglect certain things, often even ourselves.

Think about it. We begin to ignore calls while speaking with them and may not even call the person back. We pass on invites to gatherings just to keep our schedules open. We may stop what we're doing when they request a date while also spending time and money to look our best on every occasion.

Avoid doing this. Take one step at a time. Maintain a healthy balance between priorities and pleasure. A man will not neglect what matters to him; neither should women. If we do, we end up losing ourselves. The worst part is that if the relationship does not work out, we feel lost, bruised, and broken. We will often blame the other person for how much we neglected what mattered when ultimately, the enemy was our inner self.

KNOW BEFORE HELLO.

I remember someone asking me what led to my ex-husband and I becoming divorced. I simply stated that we were two good people who were not good for one another. Wow, how was that possible? I am certain that most of you reading this have said or heard the saying "We outgrew one another." After being with different partners, I finally realized what the issue was. I selected suitors based on the surface. Not their surface, but mine, because I did not know the depth of who I was.

I encourage you to take time and get to know yourself, love yourself, and accept yourself before getting to know another person. This is primarily important after a long-term relationship but also applies to different milestones in life. We were taught how to behave, how to look, where to go, and how to think. But somewhere along the road of applying what we were taught and adapting to what we see, we lost ourselves, the actual person we were created to be, the person that possesses something unique that only he or she can give to the world.

Consider this. Are you comfortable and confident with presenting yourself to someone while expressing your needs, wants, and expectations? To do so, you need to know specific information. Sure, you can kind of know and describe these things to someone else, but trust me, a confident, self-aware person will see your uncertainty. Depending on the person, they may interpret your inability to share your authentic self as a lack of confidence, insincerity, or perhaps a bit confusing, causing them to become less interested. I know you may be thinking, *oh well, it is their loss.* But the old saying "You only get one chance to make a first impression" is true. The lack of knowledge about yourself may hinder potential possibilities.

REST WELL.

When we encourage people to get more sleep, some will say, "I will sleep once I die." Hopefully, they know that not getting enough of it will allow that resting state to come more quickly than they expect.

How you spend your time
is more vital than how you
spend your money.
Time cannot be reproduced.
Moreover, we do not know
how much remains.
Spend it wisely.

BE SURE THAT YOU ARE NOT YOUR OWN GREATEST ENEMY.

In every relationship, we are learning about ourselves and others. When a relationship of any kind is dissolved, rather than pondering who is to blame and what the other party did or did not do, begin to look within. If the common denominator in each problem, is *you*, then it may be time to search out your own heart.

Begin to consider some of the events that occurred and ask yourself what you could have done differently. Consider what your perspective was about those areas of conflict before the relationship began and what your perspective is currently. What did you learn?

Now that you are outside of the emotions that were driving your reactions, are you able to consider the other person's point of view to objectively identify your personal contribution to the negative circumstances? If you are the common denominator in the undesired outcome, then it is imperative that we pause from people and utilize that time and energy on personal development.

I know this takes time, honesty, and maturity. However, if we desire to not only go through but grow through difficult situations, we must be able and willing to self-reflect.

There are seasons in our lives that will require us to grow. Just like pruning a tree helps get rid of decay, the things in our lives that have become old, rotten, and good for nothing must be pruned away. If we miss taking the time to do this, those unfruitful areas will begin to spread and infect other areas of our lives, ultimately leading to premature death. This necessary process cultivates a prosperous life, a life that is healthy and whole in every area.

You are a tree planted by rivers of living water.

Be a wise gardener.

HAPPINESS IS NOT PRESENT BECAUSE SADNESS AND DISAPPOINTMENTS ARE NOT. HAPPINESS IS CHOOSING TO LIVE, LOVE, AND BE GRATEFUL DESPITE THEM.

My childhood was not the best or the worst. My mother became ill while pregnant with my youngest brother and ended up passing away when I was nine years old. I was the eldest of four children in my father's home and was treated more like a nanny than a daughter. My siblings were only a few years younger than me. However, it has always felt as if we were a decade or more apart. I began caring for my mother at the age of seven, and she trained me on how to care for children and a home. My life was very different from my peers, and most, if any, could not relate. I cooked my first holiday meal at the age of ten. Supporting my father by caring for my siblings was challenging to say the least, but I learned a lot of skills as a child that prepared me for the life that was ahead of me.

The Bible says that "all things work together for good to those who love God, to those who are called according to His purpose" (Rom 8:28 NKJV). Now I understand that God was preparing me for the place I was heading. He knew me, loved me, and provided for me even before I knew He was God. I grew up in a busy, poverty-stricken neighborhood on the West Side of Chicago. I had no mother, an alcoholic father, and a crack-addicted stepmother, and after years of yelling, fighting and complete dysfunction, I left home at the age of fourteen. I had my first child at the age of eighteen, but God! All the things that made me miserable as a child provided me with the wisdom, knowledge, and understanding that I needed to prevent myself from becoming just another statistic.

Listen to me. There is a purpose within the pain. Yes, it may be frustrating, uncomfortable, scary, hurtful, and discouraging, whatever *it* is. However, we grow as we go.

Having a mind that refuses to quit despite having faced everything is a mind that has persevered through much hardship. However, after the trials and tribulations have passed and we begin to apply the knowledge that we have learned, we become wise. Knowledge is knowing; wisdom is doing. I learned the most about myself, God, and my environment when I was in the lowest seasons of life.

Keep telling yourself that this is only temporary. This too shall pass. This is not the end of the book; it is only the end of the chapter. We may not choose the trials that we face, but we can choose how we face them. We can be victims or victorious. We can choose to break the cycle or be broken by it. Just keep in mind that your future self is relying on you to choose wisely.

Being an overcomer is a decision we make one trial at a time, over, and over again.

Just because you like it does not mean it is good for you. If it is not good to you, it is not good for you.

DO NOT ALLOW THE FAMILIAR AND FEAR TO PARALYZE PROGRESS.

When we become comfortable with the state that we are in, we lack the desire to try. We become complacent with mediocracy. Without adequate vision, there is no hope, and people begin to believe that there is no other way. Our minds begin to tell us we may not be where we desire, but at least we know what to expect and how to manage where we are. This manner of thinking is easy. It does not require much effort, thought, or time. Do not give in to those thoughts!

Did you know that the Bible says that our own hearts deceive us? We must practice and train our minds to only think on and believe in what is good, pure, kind, peaceful, beautiful, and holy; for me, these things are based on the word of God.

Guard your mind and heart by being intentional about what you see and hear. The eyes and the ears are the windows to our hearts. As we begin to look and listen, our minds begin to create images. Once those images are formed, our imagination is ignited. If we are not diligent and steadfast in this area, our minds will rule over us. We will become subject to whatever wavering thoughts we have. This is dangerous and will cause us to be led by evil, temptation, anger, and the like. We will begin to create ideas in our minds that are based on assumptions, illusions, fear, and other unknowns. We will end up making real-life decisions based on this imaginary state of mind.

Avoid this mind trap by allowing yourself to be challenged. Strive to learn something on purpose daily. Have discussions and partake in activities that will edify your mind, body, and spirit. Overcome fear by cultivating your faith. Apply the word of God to your life and spend time with like-minded people. Get out of your neighborhood, switch up your daily routine, and when you go out, do something different. Instead of the movies, go downtown and take pictures. Instead of going to a restaurant, find a cooking class to attend for the night. Keep your resumé updated and make time to cultivate your natural gifts by taking courses, reading books, and studying individuals who are successful in your areas of interest.

Remember, better me = better we

**If the price is peace,
it is not worth it.**

A CLOSED MIND IS UNABLE TO UNLOCK NEW EXPERIENCES!

Simply put, keep an open mind. If you have attempted several times to accomplish the same thing unsuccessfully, then what you are doing is not working. Some of the most successful people are resilient and adaptable, determined enough not to quit, and wise enough to know that there is always more to learn.

Face the areas in your life that may need to be fixed. Be honest with yourself and be humble enough to ask for help. Let go of the need to be *right* and *alright*.

Stay teachable.

JUST BECAUSE YOU CAN DO IT ALL DOES NOT MEAN YOU SHOULD.

As a mother, a full-time employee, an active minister, a person who loves people, and the founder of an organization, there is a lot that is presented to me in a single day. Yes, God's grace is sufficient in all things, and yes, we can do all things through Christ, who strengthens us (Phil 4:13 NKJV); however, we must remember that it is *through* Him.

The enemy will remind us of the scriptures I just stated and have us convinced that we are able to do each task presented to us in a day, do them well, and still have time to take care of ourselves and our homes. The devil is a liar and the father of them. One of his names is the deceiver of the brethren. Those scriptures are true. Nevertheless, knowledge is knowing, and wisdom is doing. God also tells us to lean not on our own understanding but acknowledge Him in all our ways, and He will direct our paths (Prv 3:6 NKJV). Acknowledging God in all that we do will allow the Holy Spirit to guide us through our day one task at a time. He can only guide us if we acknowledge Him. This is how we can do all things *through* Christ. So let us not be deceived. Just because we can does not mean we should.

In addition, we can save a lot of time, energy, and resources by utilizing the people that have been placed in our lives with their own gifts and talents. I am a writer and a speaker; however, I have no desire to figure out editing, design, and marketing. I am okay with seeking help in these areas. Doing so will not reduce the value of my personal contribution, nor will it reduce yours.

Let's work smarter not harder!

WHO YOU SPEND YOUR TIME WITH TODAY WILL IMPACT YOUR TOMORROW.

Two scriptures you will often hear me say are "Two are better than one" (Eccl 4:9 NKJV) and "iron sharpens iron" (Prv 27:17 NKJV). The people that we spend our time with the most, those that have regular access to our lives, reflect who we are. I did not know or believe this when I was a child. My father would tell me to stay away from certain people because he feared I would become like them. That did not make sense, and I would constantly say, "No, I am me, and they are who they are." I was not mature enough or wise enough to understand that we learn vicariously that we learn even when we are not necessarily trying to. In time, I see and know that after spending consistent time with someone, we begin to mirror their mannerisms in what we say and what we do. Therefore, choose your company wisely.

Be with them; be like them.

BE FLEXIBLE BUT BOW DOWN TO NOTHING BUT GOD!

Have an open ear to consider what others may say about a matter because you may learn something. However, keep in mind that people's perspectives are shaped by the life experiences that cultivated their point of view. If what they share does not align with your core morals and values, then you have the power to choose whether you will retain and/or reject what they are communicating. Allow yourself a moment to process the information, then allow the Spirit to guide how you manage the new data. Above all, never allow fear or other emotions to determine what you allow into your heart, mind, or life. Only God has authority over life and death, so strive to honor and obey Him above all.

YOU CAN'T REACH THE ROOT WITHOUT THE TRUTH!

When we are sincerely ready to make a change in our lives, we must not focus on treating the symptoms but on the root cause of the behavior. To do so, we must take off the mask and peel back the layers of lies that we have worn to cover up the truth. I mean, become raw and real with yourself.

Cry aloud. Say those things you have buried within you. Call out the names of those that hurt you, disappointed you, betrayed you, abandoned you, and the like. Be specific when you take time to do this. Do not simply say "Paul, you hurt me." Say "Paul, you hurt me when you ... It made me feel ... It caused me to ..."

Do not rush through this. This is a process, and it will take time. It may not be easy, but it is necessary. Your heart and mind deserve to be cleansed and renewed from the hurt. As I have stated before, we are unable to fix what we are unwilling to face. Furthermore, holding on to past hurt and pain hinders our ability to live freely. Why? Because the thoughts that stem from unresolved pain make us prisoners within our minds. The unresolved pain corrodes our hearts and corrupts new opportunities.

Think about a time you were getting to know someone. Everything is going well, and you are excited about the possibilities ahead. One day this person does or says something that reminds you of an experience, one that hurt you in some way.

It could be something minor. You had great news that you wanted to share, and when you called them, they were busy and said they would call you right back but did not call until the next day.

You rehash past letdowns within the present. Your mind begins to tell you things like *I knew this was too good to be true. I guess me and my news are not that important to them. What are they doing that is stopping them from calling or sending a text? Perhaps they are around someone they are unable to talk in front of. You know what, when they do call, I am not picking up. As soon as they call, they better have a great reason for not calling me right back or else I am done. Whenever they call, I am going to give them a piece of my mind.* Sound familiar?

In this example, unresolved trust issues have caused the heart to view everyone as suspects rather than potential partners or genuine connections that may help us in some manner. The wound of hurt oozes toxic thoughts that hinder our ability to think rationally, and we end up making poor choices that may impact our lives permanently, based on a temporary emotion, again, caused by imaginary events. An emotion that feels real and tangible because the longer we leave the hurt unresolved, the deeper it becomes, and the less we can control the effects it has on us.

Unresolved hurt is like cancer; it starts in one area of our lives and left untreated spreads throughout. It can delay our destiny due to terminating beneficial relationships prematurely and/or prevent them from being established at all. Understand that most mature individuals will protect their peace at all costs. Thus, at the sign of toxicity, they will flee from you.

Get help.

Let it go so that you can grow!

THE FACT THAT YOU ARE ASKING GOD WHY MOVES HIM TO LISTEN.

If you believe in God, do not allow anyone or anything to tell you that God is offended or enraged by your questions. God is not fragile. He is the Alpha and Omega. He is the creator of all. He is all-knowing and all-powerful. Trust that He can take our questions.

God encourages us to seek Him with our whole hearts; this includes our fears, doubts, worries, and questions. He tells us that those who ask shall be given, those who seek will find, and the door will be opened to those who knock (Mt 7:7 NKJV). As we draw close to Him, He draws close to us. Abide in Him. Rest your mind, body, and spirit by resting *in* Him. As you commune with Him, pour out yourself to Him to make room for His Spirit to fill you back up. This is how we are refreshed and renewed like the eagle.

Pause here. Close your eyes, breathe in slowly, and release slowly. Say "Lord, fill me up; You are everything, and I need a refreshing. Fill me up, and I shall be filled."

Take time to do this often to stay balanced within.

EAT TO LIVE, NOT TO FEEL.

If you realize that you use food to celebrate when you are happy, comfort you when you feel sad, or calm you when you are upset, you are most likely an emotional eater. This is more than unhealthy, and the sooner you realize this, the better.

Overcome this behavior by being intentional in your actions. When the thought of reaching for unhealthy food comes, replace it with a physical activity within your abilities; jump rope, push-ups, squats, crunches, walking, dancing, or running in place. Keep a food journal and log your feelings as often as you can, whenever you reach for food. Ask yourself, "Why am I looking for food?" Drink twelve ounces of water and wait fifteen minutes before eating to determine if you are sincerely hungry. This is a healthy tip to apply since our brains are unable to differentiate hunger from thirst.

When preparing to have a celebration, replace the high-carb sides with healthier options. Having a barbeque? Grill meat along with vegetable skewers. Prepare a colorful veggie tray and fruit tray and set up a smoothie bar with non-alcoholic tropical drinks.

We can enjoy life even more by living with purpose, on purpose.

THEY SAID THIS.
THEY SAID THAT.
BUT WHEN YOU TRULY NEED
HELP, WHERE ARE *THEY* AT?

S top concerning yourself with the opinions of those that have not invested in you, especially those who know of you but have no personal insight regarding who you are.

They do not matter unless you allow them to.

A DIAMOND HELD IN THE HANDS OF A FOOL MAY NOT BE APPRECIATED BUT DOES NOT DEPRECIATE EITHER.

Growing up I often heard people say, "Fake it until you make it". At that time in life, it made sense to me. If you do not have something and you are not in the position in life that you desire to be, simply pretend. Spend the money you do have buying things that make you *look like* you are not struggling. We read magazines to keep up on trends, become familiar with expensive clothing brands, watches, shoes, perfumes, and cars. I never missed an episode of the popular television show *Lifestyle of the Rich and Famous* hosted by Robin Leach. The show always ended with the line "Champagne wishes and caviar dreams", meanwhile we grew up chasing money to look like champagne though we were living on a beer budget.

Shun from doing this. You will waste time, money, and energy on meaningless material items. Utilize your resources to invest within yourself. There is nothing wrong with wanting nice things, traveling the world, and enjoying new experiences. However, we must understand the meaning of value and worth. Many of the things that we can see, that can be destroyed, replaced, and duplicated, are not what gives us our personal value. Your unique self, your personal morals, judgement, love and kindness for others, along with keeping your word, standing up for what is right, your willingness to help others, your creative abilities, your positive attitude, your gift of giving, ability to be fair, showing up on time, never giving up on those you love, pushing yourself beyond what others expect of you, and choosing to do right when you think nobody is looking; this is who you are. This is what makes you useful and irreplaceable.

These things can be seen, but not because you purchased them, but because these are characteristics built within your soul, and we see them in the things that you do naturally.

Know that your worth is personal and internal. Watch a jeweler complete a diamond appraisal. Very little time is spent on the outside because if the center has too many flaws, not much else matters. Take time to build yourself up internally. What we know and what we believe cannot be taken from us; it makes up the core of who we are. Only the people that we *allow* to see within will know and appreciate our true value; even if they do not appreciate you, their opinion of you does not impact the weight of your worth. Therefore, I reiterate how critical it is to know thyself. When we *know* and understand who we are and what our value is, we will not allow others to treat us as anything less than a rare gem. Their ignorance will be their loss.

Know that you are worth more than a diamond!

You may be only one person, but to one person you may represent an entire group. Always represent well.

FAITH MAKES ALL THINGS POSSIBLE; NOT TRYING MAKES NOTHING POSSIBLE.

We and the world we are in will never know how amazing we are until we are willing to push past being mediocre, go beyond doing just enough to get by in life, and press into our purpose with every part of who we are. We must pursue our destiny unashamed, relentlessly, determinedly, intentionally, fearlessly, humbly, and expect great success. We must press forward even when we are tired. We must pursue even while we are facing adversity and disappointment.

Having faith means believing that things shall be as we see in our minds and believe in our hearts, the things our eyes are yet to see. When we believe that something shall come to pass, we think, speak, behave, and work toward the expected end. Therefore, having a vast imagination is vital to achieving great success. Imagination allows us to discover innovative ways to resolve issues and create things beyond our understanding. Don't be discouraged, not everyone that you share your dreams with will understand what you're pursuing; it is not necessary that they do. What matters is what you believe.

Faith, one of the greatest reasons why we do anything.

Use computers and the internet. Do not allow them to use you. Do not waste time watching others take chances and influence change. Minimize idle screentime and maximize your life.

DO NOT ALLOW ANYONE'S ACTIONS TO DETERMINE YOUR REACTION. STAY TRUE TO WHO YOU ARE.

People have a way of pulling the petty out of us. When someone behaves in a manner that is provoking you to react in a way contrary to how you would normally react, and how you want to be remembered, practice the power of pause. Consider the outcomes if you were to react to and participate in the foolishness that is being presented to you. Often people who are quick to behave in this manner *believe* that they don't have much to lose. They are likely living day to day, have no plans, and are not assuming responsibility for themselves, let alone for anyone else. Consider your family, your faith, and your future. Pride, arrogance, and anger comes before a great fall. To some spectators you may appear cowardly, or foolish, for just walking away; however, you must know who you are and not waiver in the face of anything.

You are blessed and highly favored. You are the head and not the tail; above only, and not beneath. You are chosen. You are the curse-breaker of your family. You are the plot twist that will forever change your bloodline for good. Respond wisely or not at all.

You cannot *afford* to react in that way; it may cost you everything you have.

TO TRY AND FAIL IS LIFE. A SLOW DEATH IS WONDERING WHAT IF...

Once I was divorced, I spent months thinking not about my x's but about the y's. Why did I not finish school? Why did I not continue to visit my family in the city once I got married? Why did I stop making time for my friends? Why did I not prioritize my health once I became a wife and mother?

Listen to me, please. Gaining a spouse, children, a career, or anything else, does not mean you have to let go of yourself and what is inside of you. On the contrary, what we choose to connect to should enhance, not dilute, who we are. You were created with a unique gift to sow into the world. Do not allow your gift to go unused, undiscovered, unappreciated, and unenjoyed. Do not die with all your greatness left inside of you. If the person you are with expects you to lay yourself down to hold them, run Forrest run!

Sow, reap, repeat!

Walk in truth or fall from lies.
It's all a matter of choice.

SEASON YOUR WORDS BEFORE YOU SPEAK IF YOU WANT THEM TO BE DIGESTED.

I always prided myself on being honest, wise, and bold. However, I was too immature to realize that just because a thought comes up does not mean it is appropriate to let it out.

Consider this. When someone is yelling at you and or using derogatory words toward you, are you listening to them? If you have the gift of hearing, we hear them, but are we listening? Most likely not.

If we truly have something valuable to say, we owe it to ourselves and the listener to consider when and how to express what is within. First, pause to consider the purpose of the point you want to make. Then, think if it will provide a resolution or give understanding, and take the time to ensure that the words spoken are tactful, timely, and delivered with good intention. Anything that does not meet the above condition should be reconsidered.

Remember, we do all things *on purpose, with purpose.*

People are like a box
of chocolates.
With some, the more you get,
the more you want.
With others, just a single
taste is enough.

If you find yourself
wondering where you stand
with someone, you should
begin walking...
(Away that is)

WRITE IT AWAY.

Journaling is therapeutic. It is like taking our minds to the laundromat. It allows the mind to wash out the residue from the day. It helps our mind sort through piles of information, allowing it to decide what to hold on to and what to let go of.

Journal often for mental health.

Do not miss the beauty in living today by rushing toward tomorrow.

GOOD HEALTH IS WEALTH, SO TAKE CARE OF YOURSELF.

I know it is easy to neglect yourself when you are responsible for other people and things. However, we cannot give our best when we are not being our best. Taking time for yourself is not selfish; it is necessary.

Around the age of forty, my body began to change. I gave birth to my last child at the age of thirty-five, my metabolism was no longer the same, and I developed Hashimoto's disease, a thyroid disease. This, along with a sedentary career, led to me gaining weight. When I first noticed it, I recall saying to myself, "Jamie, lose the weight now. Do not wait to receive some horrible diagnosis before you begin taking care of yourself. It will be simple. Reduce carbs, cut refined sugars, and go to the gym." Now, six years later with a touch of arthritis, and thirty pounds heavier, guess who regrets not following the sound, loving counsel from the spirit speaking to me? Yup, this lady. I will take care of myself. I will get rid of the excess weight and readjust my relationship with food. However, I now must work with this pain, making it a bit more difficult.

Let us renew our minds by adjusting the way we see things with respect to our health. We should work out, eat foods that will adequately replenish and repair our bodies, and intentionally, get proper rest. We do this not because we need to, or because we don't like our bodies and how we feel, but because we love, appreciate, and value our bodies. Thus, we *want* to take care of our bodies. These bodies have taken care of us since we left our mother's womb.

For years, we have eaten what we wanted, stayed up all night, consumed alcohol, and indulged in smoking. Some extreme athletes have pushed their bodies beyond their limits, more than most people could ever imagine, and their bodies took the beating and kept on ticking.

However, as we grow older, it is important to avoid taking our health for granted and begin to repay our body by taking care of ourselves.

This is one form of self-love.

Before social media and until this day, that darn nobody was responsible for spreading gossip. Whenever you tell somebody to tell nobody your secret, everybody still finds out. So, if you want to keep a secret safe, don't tell *nobody*.

FAITH WILL CAUSE FEAR AND ALL ITS FRIENDS TO FLEE. I ENCOURAGE YOU TO *CHOOSE* TO BELIEVE IN GOD.

In my walk of faith, I have learned that the only constant in life is Christ, so I choose to be consistent in the one constant, Christ Jesus. He will never leave nor forsake. His love is everlasting, and His word is the same yesterday, today, and forever. He knows all of me and loves me despite me. No matter how many times I have turned my back on Him, He welcomed me back unto Himself without hesitation, repeatedly. It took more than twenty years to surrender all to Him, but my life has never been the same. I have joy, peace, and a power that rests in me that is indescribable.

Try Him; you will not be disappointed.

A PERSON IS UNABLE TO CORRECT AN ISSUE THAT IS UNKNOWN TO THEM.

If something is bothering you, speak up or accept it, but do not become upset with a person if you have not communicated that you have an issue with something that they are or are not doing. It is immature and unfair to them. People are not mind readers. It is our responsibility to express our needs, wants, and concerns, no matter how uncomfortable it may be to do so.

If you are unsure about what to say, write it down first. Then, gather your thoughts and consider a clear, honest, and kind way to express your concern. When you are ready to talk about it, consider a time that suits you both, no distractions, no audience, and not in the middle of a disagreement. Keep it as concise as possible to maintain their attention. Once you communicate, allow them time to process the information. Then, when they speak, listen to understand and not to respond or defend your side.

Keep in mind that there may never be a perfect time or way to discuss a concern, but the most important thing is to simply talk about it as soon as possible. Do not allow your imagination and emotions to take your thoughts on a ride because you may not like where they end up.

AVOID THE EVIL TWINS: PROCRASTINATION AND POVERTY

Putting off tasks impacts your life span and quality of life. It typically leads to poor money management, thus reducing cash flow. Consider this. A late fee is added for missing a bill payment; further delays may cause a repo or disconnection of services. Funds initially saved for something else are now being used, thus impacting future financial goals. Putting off chores causes our workload to increase, eventually making what could have been a simple task now a difficult and time-consuming one. When we avoid making or taking a call, the result may be missed opportunities and/or delays for goods or services we need; this can become dangerous when it concerns our health, such as putting off doctor visits, medical screenings, procedures, and medication. Sadly, many people die simply due to not following up with a health concern on time.

The adage "Don't put off tomorrow for what you can do today" is a discipline that should be taught and applied as early in life as possible. Listen to me. If there is a task in front of you that you can take care of, just get it done. Practice this as often as possible, and it will become part of your character. You will be a doer with increased peace of mind. How? When tasks are left incomplete, we begin to worry about them subconsciously. Eventually, the worries begin to overwhelm our thoughts and anxiety hinders our mental health. I know firsthand that when our minds are consumed with worry, we become mentally exhausted and very little gets done, which only wreaks more havoc in our lives and relationships.

If you are a procrastinator, there is hope, but you must be able to see and admit that there is an issue. Unless we see a problem, we will be unable to commit to a solution.

Make the intentional choice to live and do everything on purpose. Practice completing tasks one by one. Remove known distractions. Make a daily to-do list and complete the least favorite or most challenging thing first. Take short, timed breaks in between a few completed tasks. Share your to-do list with an accountability partner who is able and willing to send reminders and words of encouragement as you make progress. Alexa and Google are great tools for accountability as well. Use these devices to set reminders as well as periodic positive affirmations. Lastly, once you get in from work or completing errands if you have more to do keep those shoes on. Doing this will keep the brain in action mode. Once we take our shoes off, we are sending signals to the brain that it is time to relax.

Do not delay your destiny any longer. As Nike's slogan says, "just do it."

A CONSISTENT PERSON DOES NOT MAKE THEM THE RIGHT PERSON.

I was dating a man. He was a beautiful man inside and out. I was able to clearly and quickly identify the positive attributes that made him unique. We appreciated one another by engaging in conversations, prayers, laughter, and simply being available. I went from admiring his attributes to being irritated by everything he did.

Why? Because the only part of me that sincerely appreciated him was the broken little girl who never faced the fear of neglect and abandonment that attempted to taunt her within any intimate relationship. I was not happy; I was comfortable. I found him reassuring. I was allowing myself to be okay with simply being okay. He did not challenge me in any manner, and I enjoyed feeling adored. When you are not whole, you can talk yourself into accepting *anything* just to have *something*.

You see, his hourly calls, texts, and video chats comforted my fears. He never allowed my imagination to run wild because his need to be accepted, liked, and needed caused him to cater to all my needs. I knew this and allowed this to go on simply because it felt good. It was not good. It was not healthy, and it was not what my future needed. However, the broken little girl held on to the broken yet beautiful man, all because she knew that the time to heal was upon her, and she would soon have to grow up. She wanted one last turn to settle, just to see if she could be satisfied with it.

In case you need to hear this, two broken people do not equal a whole union. A lifetime union, a marriage, requires two healthy, whole people, not perfect people, but people who complement one another's lives perfectly. Two people who know, understand, and love themselves and one another despite their flaws. They can be and love organically.

When you are organic, you do things without ulterior motives. Your morals, beliefs, and desires lead your deeds. You tend to be balanced and thrive in creating win-win scenarios because you want to give and receive; you are whole. Whole people are not people-pleasers, not at the cost of their peace. Thus, whole people are typically sincere individuals. They do what they genuinely want, not to fill a void, not to feel useful, and not for kudos. This type of person is confident and trust-worthy. In my opinion, a rare gem.

If you connect with such a person, appreciate them. If you are one, never change!

A WISE BUILDER COUNTS THE COST *BEFORE* HE BUILDS.

Waiting is not a curse!

FEELINGS ARE NOT FACTS!

YOU may be the one you're waiting for. Show up for yourself.

ROCKING CHAIR SYNDROME

Do you or a loved one suffer from Rocking Chair Syndrome? Here are a few symptoms to consider:

- Making a lot of moves with little to no progress made.

- Excessive talking about dreams/ideas with no real plans or course of action taken.

- Seemingly "too busy" to complete tasks that may help get you closer to achieving your dreams.

- Watching others around you set and achieve goals, while you're still trying to figure out all the details of your vision in your head; one big idea after the next.

- A few sporadic attempts to watch videos and read books about your area of interest; becoming distracted and not finishing any of them.

- When you're alone, you often ponder on how things would be if you ever decided to follow through on anything. Sometimes feeling sad, overwhelmed, and mentally drained by just the thought of all the work that will be required for the vision to come to pass.

You don't have to suffer. Choose to live. Take a chance and invest in yourself. Do not be deceived by busy work. Like a rocking chair, there's a lot of movement, but all the while staying in the same position. Get a notebook and write your vision down. Take time to ponder on the who, what, when, where, and don't forget the why. As a matter of fact, start with why. Why do you want this business or whatever it is? Who does it help? How does it help? What talent, gifts, and skills do you have that will add value and support the vision? Don't worry, you will not have all the answers, you don't have to know everything, because others will help you along the way; people need people. You will realize that the people you may want to help you won't, but someone will. You simply must believe that with faith, work, consistency, and time you can achieve anything. Don't give up on yourself or the dream, however, you must wake up and get to work or else it will always be that—a dream!

NO MATTER WHAT HEIGHT YOU REACH IN LIFE, NEVER FORGET THE LOW POINTS THAT PUSHED YOU THERE. STAY HUMBLE.

Whenever I felt as though my back was against the wall and I did not know how I would press forward, my faith allowed me to pause and look back at what I had already made it through. I would recall places and events that occurred and be encouraged, knowing that those moments passed and made me better, wiser, and stronger than before. Furthermore, those moments in time inspired me to keep going to avoid falling back. Those hard-pressed positions fueled my nevertheless press from beyond the pity party into a praise party.

I chose to be who I was designed to be. I am more than a conqueror.

I encourage each of you to create a personal breakthrough journal. Document trials you have faced, and date the day you overcame the obstacle. Be sure to document how you felt while going through that season of life and how you felt the moment you realized you were beyond the burden. Be honest, transparent, and raw. List how you responded to God, your family, and yourself during the trial. In addition, describe how you grew through what you went through.

Hold on to the journal. Mediate on it the next time you are up against another giant. Share it with those you love, especially your children. Allow your voice to encourage your-self and others. Even when times are going well, look back and pause to praise God for every moment that has cultivated who you are today.

Each moment matters to the masterpiece, which is you.

PARENTING WISDOM AT ALL STAGES

- If possible, breastfeed your babies. Breastfeeding has many benefits for you and your baby. It creates an unmatched bond while the baby is nestled on your flesh. It builds the baby's immune system by providing natural vitamins that the body produces during lactation and helps to restore your belly. As the baby suckles, our abdominal muscles contract. Breastfeeding also burns calories.

  Do not be discouraged. Breastfeeding the proper way is not painful and does not flatten your breasts. If the baby's mouth covers most of the areola, you will have minimal nipple discomfort, and your nipples will keep their natural shape. After each feeding, use some of the dripping milk to moisturize each nipple by allowing the nipples to air dry; do not wipe.

  Remember, the more you nurse the baby, the more milk your body will produce. You can pump in between feedings and store the breast milk. Be sure to write the date on the storage bag and use the oldest milk first. It is good to have the extra milk on hand in case you must run an errand, work a bit longer, or eat something you do not want the baby to have. If this occurs, you can skip nursing, use the stored milk, pump the milk out and toss it.

  Note: When you breastfeed, the baby's poop will be yellowish and soft, which is perfectly normal since mommy's milk is natural. It is easier for babies to digest.

- I must admit, when it comes to diapers, you get what you pay for. You do not have to buy the most expensive, but if you go with the cheapest, you will find that they leak quite a bit and may be less comfortable for the baby.

- Use sensitive and fragrance-free wipes. Babies can get a rash and even yeast infections. If this happens, allow the baby to lay around with the diaper off for a bit, placing a towel or puppy pad underneath to avoid messes.

 The air will dry the rash, allowing the skin to heal faster. Keep Desitin® on hand and use it generously in those little baby fat cracks.

- As a new parent, rest as often as you can. It will help regulate your mood swings while your hormones are getting back to normal. Rest will also allow you to stay calm and relax when the baby is upset, and you are not able to figure out why. When this happens, and you have done all that you can do, it is okay to place the baby down in a safe spot and walk away for a moment to get a break from the crying. Crying is not a sweet sound and not wanting to hear it does not make you a bad parent.

- Dads, you matter. Your touch, voice, scent, hugs, and kisses help to build a bond in the baby's early days. Babies grow quickly, and you want to spend as much time as you can one-on-one. While you build that father-child bond, it also allows Mom to have a short break for herself. Whether you are together or not, you must work as a team to create a safe and healthy environment. The full-time caregiver, be it Mom or Dad, must be allowed a mental break to be stress-free so they can be the happiest, healthiest caregiver they can be.

A happy parent cultivates a happy child. You are not doing one another a favor; you are working together for the sake of the child.

- Things that help to stimulate brain growth while in the womb and outside: classical music, reading to the baby, and eating healthy foods. Yes, they are listening in the womb.

Be careful about what you allow those tiny ears to hear.

- Despite what we have seen and lived through, yelling, cursing, and harsh beatings do not resolve issues. Do not pass on the generational curse of being belligerent, demeaning, unreasonable, and/or abusive in any manner. Remember, children have thoughts, feelings, and emotions. Like us, they learn vicariously, even when they are not trying to. Their brains are truly like sponges. Even a little negative input absorbed may cause it to yield rotten mannerisms. Think about a sponge that stinks. The smell is a result of the residual waste left behind to spread. Let us not allow the waste of our unresolved issues to become our children's mess. When we know better, we must do better. Choose to be the curse breaker in your bloodline.

- Teach your children the names of their body parts. Do not use nicknames for their genitals to avoid confusing the child or making them feel that these are areas that should not be spoken of. In addition, if asked about their bodies (*by a sexual predator attempting to groom them, for example*), this kind of response will indicate that the child is being educated about body safety, hopefully, warding off a predator. *Shady People* and *My Body Belongs to Me* are good book suggestions to help discuss this topic with your child(ren).

- When your child does something wrong identify the issue, talk, and listen. Discuss the concerns, expectations, consequences, and solutions. Help them learn conflict resolution tactics early so that it becomes natural for them. Of course, this will vary depending on age. A spank on the bottom may be necessary now and again but should not be the first or only method of correction.

- Teach your children to clean up behind themselves, make their beds each morning, and exercise—along with other good habits—at a young age. It will cultivate structure, discipline, and positive habits for life. In addition, doing this early on will ensure that good habits are incorporated into their routine, becoming a way of life rather than a chore.

- To the best of your ability, make sure your children receive regular physical, eye, and dental exams. Ask questions and engage the children by asking if they have any questions and/or concerns you may have missed. It will allow them to become comfortable speaking about their bodies and health concerns. Any new information obtained by the doctor should be discussed with the child after the exam to check for understanding. In addition, complete allergy testing early to avoid any serious allergic reactions. Communicate the findings with the children and explain any serious concerns. Do not worry; this is not too much for them. Children are like sponges and will retain this vital information. Lastly, please ensure you know whether your child carries the sickle cell trait. They will need to know this, especially as they get older and begin to date. Remember, the trait itself may have little impact. However, having a partner with the trait will birth a child with sickle cell, which should be avoided if possible.

Encourage them to discuss this with anyone they become interested in so they can decide how to move forward before things become serious.

- From birth and beyond, be mindful of what your children see and hear you doing, especially between parents. Avoid arguing, name-calling, and the like. You cannot tear one another down and expect the child to respect you afterwards. As adults, even if we forgive and move forward, those little hearts remember and may become resentful.

  The observed behavior also lays a foundation regarding what is acceptable in life. Before you do anything consider what you would want your child to view as "normal" in life.

- Cultivate generational blessings rather than curses. Do this by living intentionally and teaching your children along the way. Admit when you are wrong and share age-appropriate lessons that you have learned throughout life because of past mistakes. This will give them the opportunity to avoid those same errors, while allowing yourself to be seen as imperfect and vulnerable. This is true intimacy, (*into me see*). Perhaps share how your childhood was and provide them insight regarding why you may respond or see things the way that you do. Taking the time to do this when applicable will create a solid, lasting bond, in addition to allowing them to understand the power of choices and consequences. Lastly, this creates a safe place for them to confess their own faults as various instances occur that will allow you to support them and hold them accountable for their actions, always reminding them that we are all a work in progress, and that discipline cultivates good character.

- Please remember, your child is a part of you, but they are not you. They are their own unique person. Keep this in mind when speaking to them after they have done something contrary to what you may have taught them and far from how you may have handled the situation. Avoid making statements like "*I would have never done. . .*" or "*When I was your age, I . . .*" As a parent, we are not cultivating clones. We are teaching and training unique individuals.

- Parents, I know we want our children to experience a life better than ours. However, we must define "better." If we consider a better neighborhood, is the one we have in mind culturally diverse and safe? Is the neighborhood a place where your children can go outside and play with peers and build social skills and relations with people from similar and various backgrounds? Or will they be the unicorn of the neighborhood and classroom? I have seen firsthand how being one of a kind (race/culture) may cause anxiety, identity issues, and low self-esteem and lead to ridicule, bullying, ostracism, and even suicide. Consider all things while choosing childcare providers, where to live, and where to attend school.

- Please understand this. If you are the non-custodial parent, the parent that lives outside of the home, it can be challenging to build and maintain a bond with your child(ren), but it is worth it. Investing time, love, care, money, and patience into our children is an investment that will yield a prosperous return.

- Take the time to talk to your children. Listen to your child to sincerely learn about them and understand their viewpoint on the topics you discuss. There will be cues during the conversation that will enlighten you about their character, concerns, strengths, and opportunities. Ask follow-up questions if something is not clear, and if the conversation reaches a place that requires more time than what you have, suggest a pause and be sure to set up a follow up time to finish the discussion. This will reaffirm how important they are in your life.

- As a parent of four children varying in ages from twenty-seven to eleven, along with helping my father raise my siblings since I was the age nine, I have learned a lot over the years. A very important aspect of any relationship is communication. I know how heartbreaking it is to receive news from your child that goes against what you believe in and what you expect from your child. However, to teach and train them in the way they should go, they must trust us. Trust is developed over time; through various experiences we share. As challenging as it may be, and trust me at times it will be, cultivate a space that your child feels safe to speak honestly in. When the child has something to share that may be a bit scary to discuss with you due to possibly disappointing you, encourage them to schedule a sharing is caring session. This is a non-judgement time of counsel. Try sitting on the floor back-to-back, (use chairs if you're unable to sit on the floor) and allow them to speak freely; respectfully of course. This will prevent them from seeing your facial expressions while discussing the matter. Jot down notes while listening, not to use a weapon to throw back in their face, but to avoid missing vital information due to potentially being emotional as you process what is being shared. Note, if you are too emotional to speak, simply state something like, *thank you so much for being honest with me. That was brave and I am proud of you. Give me a moment to think about what you just shared so we can discuss the best way to move forward.* You may have to breathe through this part. This is a process that will take patience, self-control, and practice. Remember the objective. You want your child to keep you aware of what's going on in and around them. The only way you can guide them, is to know them and what they are being faced with. If they can't trust you to be there for them through difficult times

- When making choices regarding how you raise your child(ren) not everyone may agree with what you decide; this is perfectly fine. Like every other area in life, we must be willing to consider what is being shared, however, the final decision will be yours. "Every tree is known by its own fruit" (Luke 6:43-45 KJV). If the tree that is speaking has repeatedly yielded a healthy crop, then you may want to pay close attention to what is being shared. If not, be careful about what you allow to influence your opinion.

- While growing up, many of us experienced the fun of sleepovers. We stayed up late, ate junk food all night, made prank calls, and went to sleep talking about everything. Although it created lots of fond memories, please understand that there are many risks involved in allowing your child to sleep in an environment that you have limited knowledge of and little to no power over. Sleepovers may appear to be part of the norm, however, proceed with caution. I do not recommend hosting or attending sleepovers due to the amount of responsibility, time, and strategy involved. This is even more true if your home has both males and females residing in it. A few things you should know before sending your child(ren) for a sleepover are:

a. Who lives in that home and who will be present while your child is there?

b. What are the sleeping arrangements?

c. Will they be leaving home for any activities?

d. Who will be the responsible adult watching over everything?

e. Will the space you hangout/sleep in be open, or behind closed doors?

f. What is on the agenda?

Consider what a room full of children behind a closed door, with peer pressure, and without any supervision may have to partake in. No matter how smart, kind, courageous, and honest our child(ren) may be, under certain circumstances, *anyone* can make a poor decision. Proper planning, along with supervision and parental engagement helps in minimizing incidents but does not guarantee it. Sadly, molestation, rape, bullying, and introduction to drugs, alcohol, and pornography occur in such environments. It is not pessimistic, it is realistic.

Have fun, be wise, and stay safe.

DO NOT ALLOW DIVORCE TO DEVOUR THE CHILDREN

D ivorce is not easy, not fun, and typically not planned. As adults we choose to marry, we choose to have children, and we choose whether we quit. Unfortunately, like any other battle, there are casualties. However, we must do as much as we can to protect and reassure our children throughout the process. We must practice laying our differences to the side while adjusting to the new way of life and do what is best for the children.

State clearly and directly to the children that the choice to divorce has nothing to do with them; it is not their fault. They do not have to choose sides.

They are not negotiators and or mediators between parents. Avoid asking the children to relay messages. If you are unable to have respectful, verbal communication, send a text, an email, or use a court appointed liaison. Keep the children out of the petty differences and trivial discussions. Children are not spies, so avoid asking them questions regarding the other parents' life along with other affairs that to do not pertain to them specifically. Lastly, children are observant and expressive; they will share things that they see and hear. Depending on the age of the child, they will randomly share this information as it comes up in their mind. If there is someone or something you rather keep private, keep it away from the child. Although it is important for the child to understand and respect privacy and boundaries regarding each perspective household, it is equally important that the children and parents alike feel safe, secure, respected, and considered in significant matters. To maintain a trusting environment, we should not tell children to keep *secrets*. We will often hear, "*What goes on in this house stays in this house*". While I understand that some things may be embarrassing or simply private, this line of thought can make children vulnerable under certain circumstances. What if the child is being abused or mistreated in some way within *that* home? Statistics tell us that 95% of sexually abused children will know their perpetrator (*Child Protection Council, 1993*), thus, children should always feel comfortable sharing what goes on under *any* circumstance.

Divorce is difficult for everyone involved; however, as we keep what's most important in mind, we can maintain a peaceful and healthy environment where our children can thrive and have happiness.

- Do not allow anything or anyone to come in between your relationship. If you live out of state, this may be even more difficult. The best thing you can do is do your personal best. Use technology to your benefit. Create regular video chats to see them while you are speaking. Pay close attention to their body language and remove as many distractions as possible to ensure they know they have your undivided attention. These intentional actions will make them feel important and secure in the relationship. Call and text daily to stay connected and ensure you are aware of the things going on in their ever-changing lives. As the primary parent, we can be consumed with life and simply forget or grow accustomed to doing things and making decisions without the other parent. Regularly chatting with the child will help you stay ahead of things, especially once they are old enough to fully articulate things on their own.

- College will not be the route to a stable and successful career for everyone. Take time to know your child and what they are naturally good at. Trade schools offer a great alternative for those who desire to be financially independent, or even pursue entrepreneurship.

Your child may be smart; however, they may not be wired to sit in a class listening to endless lectures on information that they will use less than forty percent of. Skilled trades such as plumbing, electrician, HVAC, auto-mechanics, and hairstylists are necessary, honest, and good paying options besides attending university. Help guide your children, but the choice and conse-quence will ultimately be their own.

- If your children are into sports or other extracurricular activities, ask how things are going and if they need anything that would help them to perform at their best; do as much as you can to show them that you love them and that they matter. When children feel loved, sup-ported, and important, they are more confident and less likely to become prey to peer pressure, social media, and other external influences. When they lack these things, they begin to seek affection, validation, and security from others. Sadly, predators of all kinds can see desperation and low self-esteem a mile away and will swoop in to devour the prey.

Be your children's first hero by simply loving them.

SISTER TO SISTER

THINGS I WISH I KNEW EARLIER
IN LIFE AS A FEMALE

NOT ALL MEN THINK THE SAME!

- Appreciate being a female and embrace your femininity. Yes, we experience a lot that men do not, but these differences are why we are valuable, powerful, and irreplaceable.

- Avoid putting a razor on your skin at all costs. Use hair removal creams, wax, or other less invasive hair removal methods. They will help to avoid hair bumps, darkening of the skin, and potential scarring from razor cuts.

- After reaching the age of eight, keep a discreet emergency period bag with you. It should contain a few maxi pads, ibuprofen, a pair of undies, and a pair of leggings just in case of an accident.

- Brush and floss daily; do not forget to brush your tongue. Healthy teeth and gums begin with good oral hygiene. Nice teeth cultivate smiles and confidence.

- No matter how thin you are, exercise should be part of our daily routine, like brushing our teeth and hair. Consider walking, jogging, skating, dancing, bike riding and the like. Exercising keeps your heart strong, waist thin, stress low, and mind clear, all of which yield high self-esteem and good health. Incorporate this early, so it is not a chore but a life choice.

- Your body is a temple. It is holy ground. Holy ground is a place of reverence and not a place where anyone can explore and lay. We are valuable, and our virginity is to be held as a prized possession, only to be awarded to the one who is worthy. The one who endured the race with grace, patience, love, and integrity.

  The one who stayed the course because they understood that waiting patiently for the prize would not compare to achieving the ultimate gift, which is you.

  Consider this. Collectibles lose value as soon as the original package is opened. They are now considered used and even damaged. Do not allow yourself to be treated anything less than a one-of-a-kind collectible. My goodness, it took me a long time to learn this. It does not matter how many tricks you show in the bed, how beautiful you are, or how much money you have. If his heart does not receive you as a wife and partner, you will never be the one he weds. If you matter to a man, he will honor you and wait for you or leave and come back begging once he realizes the value of what he had. Celebrities that are admired like Beyonce, Halle Berry, Rhianna, Jlo, the Kardashians and many more have been cheated on. Liars lie, cheaters cheat.

  So, do not compromise your character.

- Moisturizer is the best friend for your face, scalp, and body. Use your middle finger to rub moisturizer around your eyes and mouth in a circular motion. These are areas where wrinkles form from smiling and frowning. Do not neglect your neck. Lean your head back and rub up and down on the skin of your neck while rubbing the lotion in.

- Take time to scrub your knees, ankles, heels of your feet and elbows while you are in the shower to keep the skin from becoming rough and dark from dirt buildup. Use body scrubs in these areas at least twice a week, along with body oil or Vaseline® to keep the skin soft.

- Regularly cutting your hair promotes growth. Avoid chemical treatments like perms and the like. Embrace your unique hair texture and use less invasive ways to rock other styles.

- Learn to admire and not envy ladies that possess something you like. Compliment them, ask for tips, and accept the things about your physical body that you are unable to change. For things that you can adjust, work on them if you really want something different.

- Ladies, we are all different. Some of us embrace a more natural look, wearing little to no makeup, while others may choose a more enhanced or glamorous look. Either way, learn to love and embrace your natural self. Your natural state reflects the creator. We are fearfully and wonderfully created in His likeness. Most importantly, avoid judging one another, potentially insulting, or hurting someone. Respect personal choice. Embrace the gift of individuality.

- Ladies, if a man does not want a committed relationship before sex, he will not want one after. If you are a born-again virgin, do not allow anyone to pressure or manipulate you into doing anything you no longer agree with. Remember, our own hearts can deceive us. Other people's hearts can deceive us too. Actions speak much louder than words. Again, if he honors you, he will honor your choice. Lastly, if you are choosing celibacy, you should be honest and open straightaway (once he initiates the conversation).

  You have nothing to lose but yourself if you are not upfront about where you stand. Above all, do not allow yourself to be in situations that will allow a mistake to happen; you will only set yourself up for failure. Keep the dates public and during the day as often as possible and set boundaries.

- Men and women think differently. As we discuss concerns with friends, their perspective may be similar, and your approach to the situation you are discussing may seem sensible because we think alike. If possible, you may want to discuss things with a trustworthy and wise male friend. This will help keep your viewpoint balanced.

- Ladies, many of us enjoy speaking. Suppose you have something important to share with your partner. Keep the conversation short and to the point. This will allow him to stay engaged and offer applicable feedback. He wants to listen; we just lose them sometimes with unnecessary details.

- I hate to break it to you ladies, but men desire a creative mind, a nurturing heart, and a loving soul, and most will also like for that to be inside of a healthy and fit woman. It is not superficial; this is *his* preference. Rather than be offended, respect his choice.

  Also, be what you seek.

- There is no excuse for not knowing how to cook. Read a book, ask Google, or watch YouTube. I do not care what he says or how well he can cook. A man does not want to get off work and come home and cook his own meal or eat at a restaurant every night. Unless you have a disability that prohibits you, get to shaking some pots!

- Men appreciate soft hands and a soft touch

- An organized home is a peaceful home. Keep your home in order; it is your sanctuary.

- The best person you can strive to be is yourself. Your gift is you. Love your unique self. The world needs the original you, not a copy of another.

- Sis, if you have a foul odor, do not attempt to mask it. Go to an urgent care center or take an at-home vaginal test to check your pH levels. When our pH is off, or we have a bacterial infection, it may cause odor. It could also be a more serious issue. Either way, do not attempt to self-diagnose. Go see a doctor.

- One of our greatest gifts is our feminine energy and its effect on the atmosphere. A soft tone of voice. The way we make our eyes speak our thoughts. The way we glide across the room, almost causing time to stand still, the ability to stay calm during a storm, and providing a soft response that tames a belligerent brute without a flinch. May our hearts heal so our femininity is restored. Ladies, let us choose feminine. Feminine is not weak. It is not subservient. It is not unequal. It is valuable, influential, intriguing, admired, desired, and necessary.

It is power; use it responsibly!

A MOMENT WITH THE MISTERS

NOT ALL WOMEN THINK THE SAME!

- We love you, need you, and desire you in our lives.

- We are not complicated. Yes, we think differently from you, but we have more in common with you then you think.

- Tell us the truth so we can trust you and know that you respect us enough to give us the information we need to make a knowledgeable decision, even if it may hurt.

  Yes, withholding information is viewed as lying.

- When we are discussing something that we are passionate about, listen to us without interrupting or without working on something else to demonstrate that you care. When you listen, it allows us to be comfortable with sharing intimate things with you. We want to be able to share things with you just like we share things with our best friends, maybe even more.

  Comfort us when we are facing difficult moments so we can be vulnerable enough to lean on you; this cultivates a bond of trust. Simply being present, giving hugs, and letting us know you are there to help are all that we may need. Do not worry about saying the right things; your actions will say enough.

- If you see us gaining weight, encourage physical activities. Working out as a couple builds intimacy. Exercise triggers the release of endorphins, which reduces stress and makes us feel happy. No matter how quickly you may burn calories, if she is watching carb intake, *you are watching your carb intake.* Support our weight goals.

  Yes, you may be okay with the extra meat to grab, but it is our body. If we are uncomfortable in our body, help us; do not hinder our efforts by minimizing our concerns in this area.

- Never allow your partner to be in a room where an ex is present, and she is unaware. Some women can be vindictive and petty, and if your current partner is caught off guard, this may cause unnecessary awkwardness. Take control by letting her know and help her feel more secure by making it clear you are together. This is especially important if your partner is attending a function with you and may not know anyone else.

- In most cases, if we have a child and our relationship does not work out, we do not want to go to court for financial support any more than you. Children cost money. Clothes, food, childcare, education, entertainment, activities, healthcare, etc. Even housing bills increase as more people use utilities. Support is needed for the child to have a decent quality of life, and the primary parent should not have to use all their resources to care for the child. Creating a child takes two people and caring for a child requires the same. If you give a reasonable amount of support based on the cost of living and needs of the child, a court is not necessary. We do not have the time, energy, or desire to deal with a court. Forget what you heard!

- If you do not want her or a child by her, do not have sex with her, period! No contraceptive is one hundred percent reliable. Only abstaining removes all chances.

  Furthermore, it is not her responsibility or your responsibility to have and use birth control, but the burden is on both parties. Sex adds additional responsibility to the relationship altogether. Therefore, pre-marital sex is discouraged.

- Men, if you are not monogamous, do not claim to be. Be honest. Know who you are and what you want, then stand on it. Your thoughts on relationships and expectations will either be accepted or rejected. You cannot miss what you have not experienced. You may be surprised how many women accept being in an open relationship. Please note that this means she is open and available to others, just as you are.

- Women admire and are aroused by a well-groomed face, nice body, and fresh scent almost as much as you admire the external beauty of a woman. We are simply less obvious about it.

- Do not believe the hype; "good guys" do not finish last. An honest, loving, respectable, and kind man may not be as appreciated much in their youth, but trust me, as soon as the relationship with the "bad boy" ends, you are her first thought and possibly biggest regret.

- Men, please go to the doctor. What you do not know may kill you. Many fatal issues can be avoided if they are detected sooner. Get an annual physical and take your meds as instructed. If you take a more holistic approach, that is fine, but follow the holistic method consistently. You matter; take care of yourself.

- If you like your partner to dress well, you may have to support that desire financially by paying for manicures, pedicures, and new hairstyles. This is especially true if she appears to be unable to keep herself up to your standards. Remember, your partner is an investment. If you see her as such, pour into her. Sow into her even without her having to ask. Believe it or not, some of us may not be comfortable with asking for help.

- Discipline your thoughts as early in your life as you can. Your thoughts should not run rampant. All that you do should be on purpose and with purpose, including thinking. A man who is unable to control his thoughts, emotions, and desires is one who cannot be trusted. This type of person will move as his passions lead him. He most likely lacks wisdom and is easily influenced. This type of man will not be respected. If a woman does not respect you, she will be unable to tolerate you and most likely will end up leaving you. If you lose respect, you lose it all.

- If she is not good enough to meet your mother, she most certainly should not meet your bed (or any bed for that matter).

  If you treat her like a clown all day long, do not consider caressing her at night. When a woman is mistreated and the mess is unresolved, your touch is despised and feels disgusting. So, until our hearts and minds are at ease, keep your hands to yourself, please.

- If you cannot afford to date, you will be unable to afford a wife. Perhaps it may be the season for you to work and save rather than seek and play.

- Remember, your encounter with a woman will shape her thoughts of man. Your inconsistencies, fears, and the like may hinder her ability to trust, appreciate, support, and/or submit to the man she is a suitable partner for. If you do not have any interest in her, do not toy with her emotions, manipulate her mind, or abuse her body. You were carried by a woman, birthed by a woman, and designed to protect, provide, and nourish her mind, body, and spirit. Whatever you invest into a woman, she will multiply it.

  If the one you encounter is not your forever, do not ruin her for another.

- Be consistent. It allows us to know that you are reliable.

- Belittling a woman that you have had a child with makes you immature, petty, and bitter. If she was undesirable, disgusting, or promiscuous why did you lay with her, and moreover, why did you lay with her without protection and plant seed in her? Remember, your partner reflects you. Consider who you associate yourself with and before being led astray by a nice face, wide hips, round bottom, and no morals, count the cost. There is a significant difference between a one-night stand and a wife.

A wife will increase your life, and a night may cost your life.

Choose wisely misters!

SECONDS
WITH SINGLES

THINGS TO CONSIDER
WHILE YOU ARE SINGLE

THERE IS A TIME TO DATE AND A TIME TO PREPARE FOR DATING.

- Single does not mean lonely.

- What is your purpose in dating? Know this and confidently share this when you meet people. They will either align or decline.

- When a long-term relationship ends, seek counseling to ensure you are whole enough to date again. We do not attract whom we want. We attract who we are. If you are hurt, bitter, angry, desperate, or broken, similar spirits will be drawn to you. Take time to heal.

- Avoid sharing all your personal business up-front. There are levels to getting to know someone. Some things are personal and intimate. If we have not progressed to a level where we are working toward becoming one, then certain topics should be kept private until the appointed time. Think about it. As we meet people and have conversations, we often disclose our employment info, educational background, number of children, number of co-parents, credit scores, the names of exes, and the reason for breakups. We go on to share our greatest fears, ultimate desires, future goals, valuable ideas, shopping and saving habits, and the like. We have handed over a snapshot of our lives to a stranger. If things do not make it past the first date, then we find ourselves doing this repeatedly.

No wonder people we have never met know all about us. We have made our lives public.

Slow down, take your time. Keep things general and only share what is necessary to have a friendly conversation while making observations. The more you grow, the more they get to know. Honestly, this will keep you safe, your reputation intact, and your heart detached.

We must intentionally guard our hearts and our lives.

- Watch how a person treats their friends and family. If someone always has something negative to say about someone and shares their loved one's personal information with you, how much more do you think they are talking about you and sharing your information?

- Listen, if you are single and your friend is married, please understand that what you share with one, you share with the other. Couples talk all day and night. If you do not want the spouse to know it, do not tell it. Yes, your friend loves you and has no intention of hurting or embarrassing you, but you must know that the two flesh became one, and they share information; yes, even when you say, "between you and me."

This may not be true for every couple, but it is for most.

- Humans like what we like. What we want, we pursue. *Nobody* is too busy to say hello or take time to see you. Especially if they claim they are interested in you.

- You will never have to ask a person how they feel about you. You will see it and know.

- If you are unable to trust them with your truth, how will you be able to trust them with your life? If you are unable to be completely open and honest with a person, they are not your person.

- If you desire marriage, but your children are your number one priority, remember, you can only have one number one priority. Know what you are ready for.

- If you do not care to answer to and or consider another person in your decision-making, then you are not ready to be in a committed relationship.

- Celibacy is not a game of cat and mouse. It is not playing hard to get or let us see how far we can go before you say no. It means do not ask or expect sex in any manner. If you do not agree, do not proceed. This is a hard stop!

- Walking down the aisle to be married is not a magical portal that makes everything better. When you say, "I do", you are saying "I do" to everything they do and *don't* do. If you desire a change, work on it, and wait on it. Saying yes is accepting the person just as they are. People may influence others, but we can't change them.

- When you go out with someone new, be sure to communicate what your plans are and who you will be with, with at least one person. Provide a picture of the person and if plans change communicate that. In addition, no matter how chivalrous a gentleman may want to be, do not allow anyone to pick you up from your home until you are comfortable.

  Your home is your refuge and should not be open to just anyone. You can meet at the place and have access to your car to leave as you wish. These days are not like the days of old. We must use caution.

- Online dating is NOT for everyone. Internet dating requires maturity, discernment, confidence, patience, discipline, wisdom, and mental stability. It can become a time thief, an unhealthy distraction if you are uncertain about what your purpose of dating is, in addition to simply creating a profile because you are bored, feeling lonely, and/or yearn attention. It should not be used to be a serial dater, using people to get out of the house knowing you are not interested in them. This is unacceptable behavior that may put you in harms way if you toy with someone's emotions. On another note, do not project yourself to be someone you are not. Catfishing may also cause you embarrassment and/or harm if you are marketing a version of you that does not exist. Put away the pictures from twenty years ago, lose the filters, and be you. If you are not comfortable in your own skin, perhaps dating isn't something to participate in during this season of life.

For better or for worse. In sickness and in health, for richer or for poorer, to love and to cherish until death do us part. Consider these vows and what they mean before presenting or accepting a ring.

Before marrying, consider this. Would you be able to care for this person faithfully and lovingly if they were unable to care for themselves? Would you trust this person to care for you as they would care for themselves if necessary? If you lost your memory or mental clarity, do you know them well enough to say they would treat you with care, dignity, patience, and love?

If one of you were unable to work, does the other have the ability and willingness to provide for the household? Basically, when life and tragedies happen, is this the person you willingly choose to endure them with?

Always remember one of my favorite scriptures: "Two are better than one" (Eccl 4:9 NKJV). The same two that begin a union must be the two that cultivate, maintain, and protect it. Only God is above you two. Your families and friends make their decisions based on their needs, not yours; you likewise. Your children will grow up and do the same. So never allow ANYONE between you.

Faith, family, fitness, and finances!

A WORD WITH MY BROTHERS AND SISTERS IN CHRIST

CHRIST DID NOT COME TO GIVE US RELIGION; HE CAME TO GIVE US RELATIONSHIP WITH HIMSELF AND THE FATHER. NEVER ALLOW ANYONE TO DECEIVE YOU. WE CANNOT GET TO THE FATHER EXCEPT THROUGH THE SON.

- Denominations divide.

- Souls are more important than clothes. Let us not be distracted by meaningless matters. Some people who attend church services will be sure to dress in their best, and some may sport a more casual style. Either way, if the soul is in the seat, the anointing will remove every burden and destroy every yolk. Furthermore, a pair of pants on a woman cannot hinder the word and work of the Lord. We are called to dress modestly. Modesty has more to do with not drawing attention to oneself, for women, especially in a sexual manner. A big hat, loud perfume, long nails, and a ton of jewelry can be just as much of a distraction, or attention-seeking, as a pair of pants. Let us focus on what matters, giving God glory and demonstrating love between one another.

- There may be times when we see someone in church, and our initial human response may be to judge what we see. However, we must keep in mind that we do not know what the person next to us had to go through just to get to the building. The loss of a loved one, a layoff, a divorce, abuse, addiction, and the like. Jesus tells us that only the *sick* need a doctor. If the sick need a doctor, and Jesus is our healer, the great physician, shouldn't we *expect t*o see the drunkard, the prostitute, the drug-dealer, the dope-fiend, the liar, the sexual immoral, and all the rest?

  The day we truly get this part, is the day that the church will multiply daily, as it did in the *Book of Acts* as the Apostles preached the good news.

  Less *saying,* and more *praying.*

- God loves a cheerful giver. One who is allowed to give freely, without pressure, without judgement or manip-ulation, will always give more than expected. Let us not use fear tactics and manipulation of scriptures to invoke giving. When God gives a vision, he will make provision for it to come to pass. Trust God in every-thing. He will never leave us nor forsake us. He is our provider and will provide for every one of our needs.

- In the book of Jeremiah, the Lord told Jeremiah the specific purpose of and plan for his life. The Bible tells us that our gifts and talents will make room for us and bring us before great men. As we spend time with the Lord, the Lord will reveal what our individual gifts and talents are. He will also provide instructions to us and encourage us during times of despair. Do not waste time envying what others do well, nor thinking how they are blessed by working their gifts. This communicates to God that we are not satisfied with the gifts He has endowed us with and are not happy with the increase He has supplied. Imagine saving up and buying a gift that you just knew would wow your child on Christmas day. When the child finally opens the gift, you don't see the reaction you expected, and he/she tosses the gift aside, pouting over what a sibling received, and begging to play with what doesn't belong to them. It shows a lack of care, value, and appreciation. How would you feel knowing the time, energy, effort, and resource that went into handpicking just the right gift?

In the same manner, God is a jealous God. He shall get the glory in all that He does. Although our gifts come without repentance, meaning God does not repent over the gifts He has given, thus He will not take them back, our gifts can go dormant; good for nothing.

If you have shown lack of care and appreciation toward your gifts, repent and move forward. It is better late than never to be faithful over all that God has given. As we are faithful over little, God will allow us to be rulers over much.

- Faith without works is dead. Faith is an action word. When we believe something shall become we operate in that expectation. Our belief that a thing shall come to pass, will cause us to put the work in faithfully, causing it to manifest. When it feels like you have done all that you can do, keep pressing. In due season, you shall reap if you faint not. Remember, the runner is most exhausted just before crossing the finish line.

You can feel tired and discouraged; however, do not allow those feelings to hinder your faith.

Press into your purpose!

- Iron sharpens iron, and a companion of fools will suffer harm. God takes us from faith to faith and glory to glory. When it is time to grow, there may be people, places, and things that we must let go of. Those familiar things may cause us to become complacent, satisfied, and may make us feel accomplished. We will never know the depth of what we can do until we are faced with unimaginable challenges. Trials and tribulations build faith, character, strength, endurance, and patience. They also reveal who is truly for us and who has only been around to glean from our gains.

A true friend speaks the truth in love; fake friends tickle our cars with flattery, and then, laugh at our foolish choices. True friends remind us of who God created us to be; fake friends encourage us to be who they need us to be.

A true friend will protect your secrets even if they are upset; a fake friend will listen to gossip and add to it. Remember, there will be a friend that sticks closer than a brother, and misery loves company. Let go of misery and move forward into your blessed future.

- God's word is true, not man's interpretation of it. Read and study the word for yourself. Ask the Holy Spirit to teach you the meaning of the scriptures. When we seek Him, we shall find Him, and John 1 tells us that God is His word. Build your relationship with Him by reading the word daily. Like a natural relationship, the more time we spend with Him, the more familiar we become. Over time, we build trust and understanding.

  The more we know, the greater our love will grow.

- Praying is how we communicate with God. Reading His word is how he communicates with us. Take time to read and pray. Communication cultivates *relation-*ship. During communication we receive revelation. Revelation provides the information necessary to cause restoration and ignite transformation, which allows the manifestation of God's promises to occur.

  We may not always trust the process, but trust that God is with us throughout it.

- We should not pay for prayer or a prophetic word. However, the worker is worth their keep, thus, give an offering to the servant of God as you are led to give, but there should not be a fee charged. Those who have been called and chosen to preach the gospel and serve God and his people sacrifice themselves to study His word, pray, fast, teach, preach, counsel, along with encouraging and supporting families for various services such as weddings and funerals; just to name a few duties.

Jesus instructed the apostles to go and preach the gospel, town to town, and not to take a purse of silver or gold, clothing, or anything with them. They were to expect and receive support from those that they served. Give honor to those that are deserving and give offerings to those that labor in the church. It would be foolish to expect a harvest when there has not been any seed sown.

In the natural, do we work for free, or do we expect to receive wages?

So, in the natural, also in the spirit.

(Read Matthew Chapter 10 for additional information).

Let's reason with one another about this topic. To maintain perspective, how many houses and cars does one servant require? The Bible says, The Lord detests dishonest scales, but accurate weights find favor with him, (Proverbs 11:1 NIV). We must consider this as leaders. We are the example. Unequal distribution of wealth is what the world looks like.

Why does the church look the same? I can make an offering as a visitor and cash app tithes as a non-member; however, I must complete several forms if I need assistance with food or help with utilities. Widows and Orphans are forgotten. This ought not be. Yes, to maintain order there must be guidelines in place. Those lines should also ensure that the people and community that the church is in, and serves are also provided with the resources and tools to cultivate hope, stability, and unity. Living well while loving and serving the Lord is one thing. Greed is another, and a form of idolatry. Money is not the root to all evil but the love of it is.

Let's strive to obtain and maintain balance in this area.

God did not design perfect men. However, He is a perfect God that can take an imperfect man with a willing heart to perform miracles. King David was an example of this. A liar, a murderer, and an adulterer, yet God called him a man after his own heart. How can this be?

As human beings, we read his life's story and shake our heads, point our fingers and gasp in disbelief; yet he was hand-picked by God (*Be careful of rejecting and judging who God has chosen*). Small in stature, but mighty in faith. Far from perfect, but he *believed* God with his *whole* heart.

He believed that despite being a scrawny, young shepherd boy, he could kill a giant that all the *strong* men feared, simply because the only true, living, and wise God was *for* him. He believed God when He said he was with him wherever he goes and would cut off all his enemies from him. Despite his poor choices, he believed God would make his name greater than any man on earth, and after his passing, would establish his kingdom from his own flesh that would endure forever. But how could David trust this to still be true after all the wrong he had done? Because God said it, and he is not a man who would lie, nor the son of man that should repent. God is God all by Himself, and next to him there is none. When we confess our sins and repent, God means it when he says he throws our sins in the sea of forgetfulness. *We should do the same.* David truly believed God, and knew he was nothing without him, which means God's Word was not contingent on David's doings. God's promises are yes and amen.

If we trust God with our whole hearts and do not doubt, confess our sins one to another so that we can be whole, and repent of our evil ways, God will receive us unto himself repeatedly. Why? Because He is faithful and true. His anger lasts but a moment, but his mercy endures forever.

If the great I Am, the creator of all, forgives us, why is it so hard to forgive one another? Who are we to judge a man, when only God knows the heart?

Trust God, love him and one another. By this, the world will *know* that we are his disciples.

Love is not something said, it is something shown.

Be encouraged, midnight only last for a minute.

ACKNOWLEDGMENTS

I would like to take the time to acknowledge everyone that God has allowed to be a part of my journey in life. Above all, He Himself. The creator of all, who kept me in all my ways and loved me when I did not love myself. He who has allowed every intricate part of my life to work together for His glory and my good.

To my family—Andresen, Davis, Davison, Powell, Thompson, and Hill, I love you all no matter how much we know of one another and despite how often we are afforded time to spend together. We are family, period; I am blessed to share blood and/or memories with you all. I am unable to make up for lost time and the events I missed in the seasons before. However, I am grateful for the opportunity to be reconnected now.

To every mother figure, my angels that were sent strategically by God during the most difficult seasons of life. You know who you are. Thank you! There are several, and to avoid missing anyone, I will not name you individually, but please know that I love you, honor you and your decision to love more than just your own. It has made a difference. I always say that there is power in a positive seed; you each were the seeds that cultivated the tree that is me.

To the sisters that God allowed me to handpick, my goodness, my sisters from the same Mister (God), I love you. Through the ups and downs, lessons, and blessings, you have been here. You have had an up-close and personal view of my heart and spirit, yet we are still here together. Stay encouraged; our best days are ahead.

To the beautiful souls that chose to sow on good ground, obeying God and believing in the gifts He has given me, enough to ensure this first of many books was published, I pray that you each continue to reap a bountiful harvest in the areas in which you need.

Lastly, to my Pastor Betty Starks of Loving Word Outreach Ministries, thank you for being an example of a servant leader. Not perfect, but faithful, loving, and authentic. God used you to reignite the fire within my spirit. You heard and obeyed Him. You spoke life into the depths of me that waxed cold. Stay the course, the lambs need you.

I love you and honor you.

Thank you all!

Remain hopeful. Our best days are ahead of us!

ABOUT THE AUTHOR

Jamie A Thompson is a mother of four and an ordained minister, born and raised on the West Side of Chicago. At the age of nine, Jamie assumed the primary care of raising her younger siblings due to her mother passing away early from illness. This changed Jamie's life forever, causing her to experience various trials and tribulations due to carrying the responsibilities and pressures of an adult, beyond what one could imagine at such a tender age.

Jamie would soon discover that God would take the palette of pain to create an amazing masterpiece like Ladies of Grace Chi, a women's organization founded on July 3, 2020. This vision was birthed with the goal of rebuilding the concept of unity and community: one woman, one family at a time. Jamie encourages women to discover and develop their individual gifts and talents, using them to teach and support one another. The idea of "a better me is a better we" inspires women to pour into themselves that which they often pour into those they love and care for.

Even while staying busy raising her siblings and assuming a life of an adult at such a young age, Jamie was still able to discover a love for reading. She read anything she could find and found that reading allowed her to escape her own reality and showed her a life beyond what she saw and experienced. Her love for reading also led her to discover her love for writing. She wants others to be ignited and encouraged by reading books like she was.

After God, Jamie's greatest passion is people. Life's trials cultivated her ability to transform pain into purpose. She was awarded knowledge and wisdom after going through and growing through these experiences. Through her writings, she hopes to provoke critical thinking and self-reflection that ultimately will motivate others to pursue inner healing that leads to a better self.

That is the inspiration for this first book.